Tools
Search
Notes
Discuss

MyReportLinks.com Books
Go!

WYOMING

A MyReportLinks.com Book

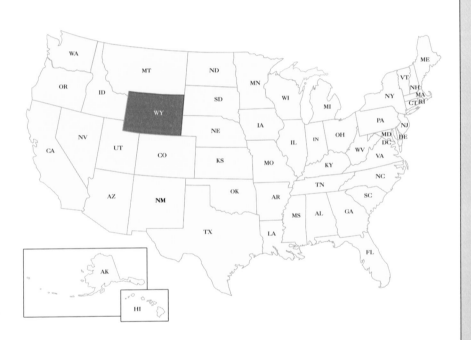

Stephen Feinstein

MyReportLinks.com Books
an imprint of
Enslow Publishers, Inc.

Box 398, 40 Industrial Road
Berkeley Heights, NJ 07922
USA

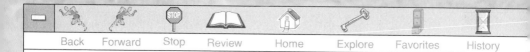

MyReportLinks.com Books, an imprint of Enslow Publishers, Inc. MyReportLinks is a trademark of Enslow Publishers, Inc.

Library of Congress Cataloging-in-Publication Data

Feinstein, Stephen.
  Wyoming / Stephen Feinstein.
    p. cm. — (States)
Summary: Presents information on the history, geography, economy, and government of Wyoming. Includes Internet links to web sites.
Includes bibliographical references and index.
  ISBN 0-7660-5030-0
  1. Wyoming—Juvenile literature. [1. Wyoming.] I. Title. II. Series:
States (Series : Berkeley Heights, N.J.)
F761.3.F45 2003
978.7—dc21

                            2002014702

Printed in the United States of America

10 9 8 7 6 5 4 3 2 1

To Our Readers:
Through the purchase of this book, you and your library gain access to the Report Links that specifically back up this book.

The Publisher will provide access to the Report Links that back up this book and will keep these Report Links up to date on www.myreportlinks.com for three years from the book's first publication date.

We have done our best to make sure all Internet addresses in this book were active and appropriate when we went to press. However, the author and the Publisher have no control over, and assume no liability for, the material available on those Internet sites or on other Web sites they may link to.

The usage of the MyReportLinks.com Books Web site is subject to the terms and conditions stated on the Usage Policy Statement on www.myreportlinks.com.

In the future, a password may be required to access the Report Links that back up this book. The password is found on the bottom of page 4 of this book.

Any comments or suggestions can be sent by e-mail to comments@myreportlinks.com or to the address on the back cover.

Photo Credits: Bureau of Land Management in Wyoming, p. 37; C. M. Russell Museum, p. 16; © Corel Corporation, pp. 3, 10; © 1995 PhotoDisc, pp. 20, 22, 23, 24; © 1999 PhotoDisc, pp. 11, 26, 35, 44; Enslow Publishers, Inc., pp. 1, 18; Library of Congress, p. 3 (Constitution); MyReportLinks.com Books, p. 4; PBS, p. 39; Sacred Land Film Project, p. 33; The Crime Library, p. 42; University of Virginia, p. 14; Women of the West Museum, pp. 29, 31; Wyoming Tales and Trails, pp. 13, 40.

Cover Credit: © 1995 PhotoDisc

Cover Descripton: Grand Teton National Park

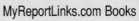
Contents

MyReportLinks.com Books
Great Books, Great Links, Great for Research!

MyReportLinks.com Books present the information you need to learn about your report subject. In addition, they show you where to go on the Internet for more information. The pre-evaluated Report Links that back up this book are kept up to date on **www.myreportlinks.com**. With the purchase of a MyReportLinks.com Books title, you and your library gain access to the Report Links that specifically back up that book. The Report Links save hours of research time and link to dozens—even hundreds—of Web sites, source documents, and photos related to your report topic.

Please see "To Our Readers" on the Copyright page for important information about this book, the MyReportLinks.com Books Web site, and the Report Links that back up this book.

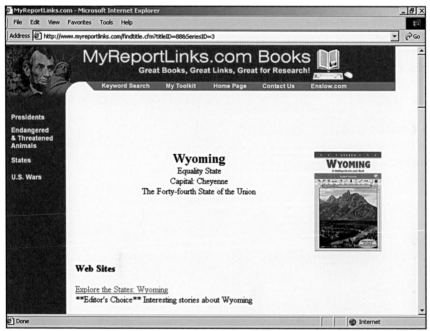

Access:

The Publisher will provide access to the Report Links that back up this book and will try to keep these Report Links up to date on our Web site for three years from the book's first publication date. Please enter **SWY8371** if asked for a password.

Report Links

 The Internet sites described below can be accessed at
http://www.myreportlinks.com

*EDITOR'S CHOICE

▶ Explore the States: Wyoming

America's Story from America's Library, a Library of Congress Web site, tells the story of Wyoming. Here you will learn basic facts about the state and find stories about cowboys and a geyser named Old Faithful.

Link to this Internet site from http://www.myreportlinks.com

*EDITOR'S CHOICE

▶ Buffalo Bill Historical Center

At the Buffalo Bill Historical Center you can visit the Buffalo Bill Museum. Explore the center's many holdings, including a virtual tour of the New Draper Museum.

Link to this Internet site from http://www.myreportlinks.com

*EDITOR'S CHOICE

▶ Lewis and Clark

PBS provides a comprehensive Web site about Lewis and Clark. Here you will learn about their travels, members of the their corps, their legacy, and much more. There are also many useful maps.

Link to this Internet site from http://www.myreportlinks.com

*EDITOR'S CHOICE

▶ US Census Bureau: Wyoming

The United States Census Bureau provides quick facts about Wyoming's population, economy, and geography.

Link to this Internet site from http://www.myreportlinks.com

*EDITOR'S CHOICE

▶ Wyoming Welcomes You

At the official Web site of the state of Wyoming, you can take a virtual tour of the state, learn about Wyoming's state symbols and history, and visit the governors office.

Link to this Internet site from http://www.myreportlinks.com

*EDITOR'S CHOICE

▶ Yellowstone National Park

The National Park Service Web site offers a brief overview of Yellowstone National Park. Click on "InDepth" to learn about the history of the park and to take an online tour.

Link to this Internet site from http://www.myreportlinks.com

Report Links

The Internet sites described below can be accessed at
http://www.myreportlinks.com

▶ **American Visionaries: Thomas Moran**
Explore the life and art of Thomas Moran and see how he was inspired by
Yellowstone Park and the Grand Canyon. You can also visit the image gallery
to view Moran's paintings.

Link to this Internet site from http://www.myreportlinks.com

▶ **Bureau of Land Management Wyoming—Historic Trails**
Historical articles about Wyoming's portion of the Oregon Trail, the Mormon
Pioneer Trail, the California Trail, the Pony Express Trail, and the Cherokee
Trail are provided.

Link to this Internet site from http://www.myreportlinks.com

▶ **Butch Cassidy and the Sundance Kid**
This in-depth article about the lives and careers of Butch Cassidy and the
Sundance Kid attempts to make sense of the conflicting facts and myths of
their much-heralded crime spree and demise.

Link to this Internet site from http://www.myreportlinks.com

▶ **C. M. Russell Museum, Great Falls, Montana**
The online home of the C. M. Russell Museum holds the biography of the
artist, writer, historian, cowboy, Charles M. Russell. The site also contains
images of him, his work, information about the permanent collection,
exhibits, and other museum facts.

Link to this Internet site from http://www.myreportlinks.com

▶ **Custer Battlefield Historical & Museum Association**
Here you will find a wealth of information about the Battle of Little Big
Horn, George A. Custer, Sitting Bull, Crazy Horse, and others involved in
the Indian Wars fought in the Black Hills.

Link to this Internet site from http://www.myreportlinks.com

▶ **Devils Tower History**
At this Web site you can explore the history of Devils Tower National
Monument. You will also find stories and learn about sacred rituals performed
at Devils Tower by American Indian tribes.

Link to this Internet site from http://www.myreportlinks.com

Report Links

The Internet sites described below can be accessed at
http://www.myreportlinks.com

▶ *Encyclopedia Americana:* **Teapot Dome**

This article explains the Teapot Dome scandal, a scandal which took place during the Harding Administration involving naval petroleum reserves in Wyoming and California.

Link to this Internet site from http://www.myreportlinks.com

▶ **Fort Laramie**

The National Park Service Web site provides a brief overview of Fort Laramie. Click on "InDepth" for a complete history of the Fort and to take a virtual tour.

Link to this Internet site from http://www.myreportlinks.com

▶ **George Catlin**

In addition to an image gallery of George Catlin's paintings of American Indians, you will also find the artist's biography, poems, quotes, bibliography, and links to other Catlin sites.

Link to this Internet site from http://www.myreportlinks.com

▶ **Grand Teton National Park Official Web site**

The National Park Service Web site provides a brief overview of Grand Teton National Park as well as its cultural and natural history.

Link to this Internet site from http://www.myreportlinks.com

▶ **Historic Sacred Sites: Medicine Wheel**

Learn about the history of the Bighorn Medicine Mountain and Medicine Wheel National Historic Landmarks and what is being done to protect them. The Web site's bibliography also contains a number of helpful links.

Link to this Internet site from http://www.myreportlinks.com

▶ **Interesting Information about Wyoming**

This Web site holds the complete text of the Wyoming State constitution, census figures, state symbols, and the state almanac.

Link to this Internet site from http://www.myreportlinks.com

Report Links

The Internet sites described below can be accessed at
http://www.myreportlinks.com

▶**PBS—The West—Red Cloud**
This biography of the infamous Lakota Indian warrior, Chief Red Cloud,
contains information about his leadership in one of the most successful
uprisings ever fought by the American Indians against the United States.

Link to this Internet site from http://www.myreportlinks.com

▶**PBS—The West—William F. Cody**
PBS's "The West" presents the biography of William F. Cody. Here you will
learn about Cody's experiences as a hunter, actor, author, and founder of
Buffalo Bill's Wild Wild West.

Link to this Internet site from http://www.myreportlinks.com

▶**Pierre Gaultier de Varennes, Sieur de La Vérendrye**
Here you will find the story of the first Europeans to set foot in Wyoming,
Pierre Gaultier de Varennes, Sieur de La Vérendrye and his sons, François and
Louis-Joseph La Vérendrye.

Link to this Internet site from http://www.myreportlinks.com

▶**Shoshone National Forest**
At the official site of the Shoshone National Forest, you will find park facts,
history, recreation information, news, and more. Navigate through the park
with the clickable maps to find information about specific areas.

Link to this Internet site from http://www.myreportlinks.com

▶**Stately Knowledge: Wyoming**
At this Web site you will find a brief listing of facts about Wyoming. You will
also find links to other useful Internet resources.

Link to this Internet site from http://www.myreportlinks.com

▶**Thomas Moran and the American Landscape**
This biography of Thomas Moran primarily focuses on the history of his
masterpiece, "The Grand Canyon of the Yellowstone," from its inception on
Moran's infamous Yellowstone adventure with Ferdinand Hayden to the
exhibition of the painting in Washington, D.C.

Link to this Internet site from http://www.myreportlinks.com

Report Links

 The Internet sites described below can be accessed at
http://www.myreportlinks.com

▶ **Travel and Tourism in Wyoming**
Here you will find Wyoming travel information, feature articles, and
news, including facts about cultural events, flora and fauna, museums,
national parks and monuments, rodeos, trails and other historic sites,
visitor activities, wildlife, and more.

Link to this Internet site from http://www.myreportlinks.com

▶ **Women's History Month Biography: Nellie Tayloe Ross**
This page contains a biography of the United States' first woman
governor, Nellie Tayloe Ross. Ross's long reign as director of the
United States Mint under the Roosevelt and Truman administrations
is also discussed.

Link to this Internet site from http://www.myreportlinks.com

▶ **Women of the West Museum—Esther Hobart Morris**
Esther Hobart Morris gained fame lobbying for Wyoming's women's
suffrage law and for becoming the first female justice of the peace in
United States history.

Link to this Internet site from http://www.myreportlinks.com

▶ **Women of the West Museum—Wyoming:
The Equality State**
Here you will learn how Wyoming became the first place in the United
States in which women were given equal voting rights and see how this
radical legislation affected the territory, its future statehood, and the
rest of the country.   *Link to this Internet site from http://www.myreportlinks.com*

▶ **Wyoming State Parks and Historic Sites**
By clicking on the images at this Web site you will find descriptions
and the history of many Wyoming state parks and historic sites. Also
included are virtual maps.

Link to this Internet site from http://www.myreportlinks.com

▶ **Wyoming Tales and Trails**
Illustrated by hundreds of historic photographs, you can learn about
Wyoming's past through dozens of folk tales, memoirs, biographies, and
historical articles. Also, the complete text of *The Virginian*, William F.
Cody's autobiography, and other works can be found here.
Link to this Internet site from http://www.myreportlinks.com

Wyoming Facts

▶ **Capital**
Cheyenne

▶ **Counties**
23

▶ **Gained Statehood**
July 10, 1890, the forty-fourth state.

▶ **Population**
493,782*

▶ **Bird**
Western meadowlark

▶ **Tree**
Great Plains cottonwood

▶ **Flower**
Indian paintbrush

▶ **Mammal**
Buffalo (American bison)

▶ **Fish**
Cutthroat trout

▶ **Reptile**
Horned toad

▶ **Fossil**
Knightia (a fish)

▶ **Dinosaur**
Triceratops

▶ **Gemstone**
Jade

▶ **Song**
"Wyoming," words by Charles E. Winter, music by G. E. Knapp.

▶ **Motto**
"Equal Rights"

▶ **Nickname**
Equality State

▶ **Flag**
The state flag was adopted in 1917. A large white buffalo appears in the center of the flag against a blue background. A red border represents American Indians and blood that was shed in battles between Indians and settlers. The state seal appears on the buffalo, as if to represent the branding of Wyoming livestock. The seal itself, was adopted in 1893.

Population reflects the 2000 census.

Chapter 1

The State of Wyoming

Wyoming, one of the Rocky Mountain states in America's West, is best known for its magnificent scenery. Not all of the state is mountainous, however. The Great Plains cover much of eastern Wyoming, and in central and western Wyoming there are flat areas called basins between the mountain ranges. The word *Wyoming* comes from a Delaware Indian word meaning "upon the great plain."

▲ *Grand Teton National Park is a major tourist spot, attracting approximately 4 million visitors each year.*

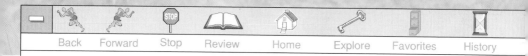
One of Wyoming's most famous attractions is Yellowstone National Park. Crowds of visitors gather each day at Old Faithful, the park's famous geyser. Old Faithful erupts approximately every eighty minutes, sending a column of boiling water and steam 150 feet up into the air.

Also in Wyoming are Devils Tower, Grand Teton National Park, and Shoshone National Forest.

Wide Open Spaces

Perhaps Wyoming's most unique quality is its emptiness. Although it is the ninth-largest state, it is the smallest in terms of population. Many Wyomingites live miles from their nearest neighbors. Even Wyoming's cities have small populations. Cheyenne, the capital and largest city, has just over fifty-three thousand people.

Almost 92 percent of Wyoming residents are Caucasian. About 6 percent are Hispanic Americans and about 2 percent are American Indians. The rest of the population is mainly made up of either African Americans or Asian Americans.

Land of the Cowboy

In addition to The Equality State, Wyoming is nicknamed the "Cowboy State." The image of a cowboy on a bucking bronco, named "The Spirit of Wyoming," appears on the Wyoming license plate and as a statue beside the state capitol building in Cheyenne.

The cowboy came to Wyoming during the 1870s. Ranchers realized that Wyoming's grasslands were excellent for grazing livestock, and so large cattle ranches were established. Agriculture is less important today, and parts of Wyoming's plains are now dotted with oil wells. The

 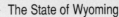
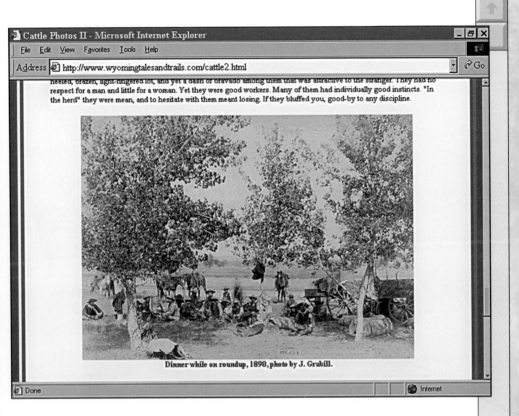

Cattle Photos II - Microsoft Internet Explorer

File   Edit   View   Favorites   Tools   Help

Address   http://www.wyomingtalesandtrails.com/cattle2.html   Go

heeled, brazen, light-fingered lot, and yet a dash of bravado among them that was attractive to the stranger. They had no respect for a man and little for a woman. Yet they were good workers. Many of them had individually good instincts. "In the herd" they were mean, and to hesitate with them meant losing. If they bluffed you, good-by to any discipline.

Dinner while on roundup, 1890, photo by J. Grabill.

Done   Internet

▲ *The life of a cowboy, while glamorized in movies, was difficult, sometimes boring, and often hazardous and dirty.*

cowboy tradition is still alive, though, and cowboys still roam the range in Wyoming, herding cattle.

In Wyoming, visitors can pretend to be cowboys. The state's dude ranches and rodeos draw large crowds each summer. During the Cheyenne Frontier Days, which last for ten days each summer, there is a rodeo every afternoon at which cowboys show off their roping and riding skills.

▶ Artists Discover Wyoming

In 1871, Ferdinand Hayden led an expedition to explore the Yellowstone region of northwestern Wyoming. With

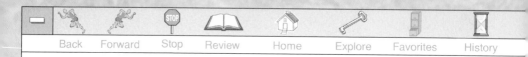
him were landscape painter Thomas Moran (1837–1923) and photographer William Henry Jackson (1843–1942). Moran and Jackson were stunned by Yellowstone's spectacular scenery. According to Hayden, the Grand Canyon of the Yellowstone River is "decorated with the most brilliant colors, the rocks weathered into an almost unlimited variety of forms."[1] He went on to say that "Mr. Moran exclaimed with a kind of regretful enthusiasm that these tints were beyond the resources of human art."[2] Even so, after returning from the trip, Moran created many paintings from his sketches, among them *The Grand Canyon of the Yellowstone.*

The Grand Canyon of the Yellowstone, Thomas Moran, 1872
Purchased by Congress in 1872; moved to the Dept of the Interior 1950
Formerly placed in Senate Lobby

Moran's vision of the west accords with that of his contemporaries. Although he took pains to portray the geology accurately, he admits that he had idealized the view of the canyon because his mission is to create art, not a topographical map. While he does render the rocks in geological accuracy, his overall purpose is to convey a personal impression of the view. The scale of

▲ Due to the influence of his paintings on both tourism and governmental action to preserve the wilds of the West, Thomas Moran was nicknamed "Father of the National Park System."

Later that year, Jackson and Moran presented their work to the U.S. Congress. On March 1, 1872, President Ulysses S. Grant signed the Yellowstone Act, creating the first national park. Mount Moran in nearby Grand Teton National Park was named after Thomas Moran.

Other artists were inspired by Wyoming's people and wildlife. George Catlin (1796–1872) sketched and painted the region's American Indians. Alfred Jacob Miller (1810–74) portrayed American Indians, mountain men, and places such as Fort Laramie. Bill Gollings (1878–1932) painted cowboys, American Indians, and ranch life in Wyoming. Conrad Schwiering (1916–86), who was raised in Laramie, is best known for his dramatic landscapes of the Teton mountains. His painting *High Mountain Meadows* was used for the centennial postage stamp for Wyoming in 1990. The abstract expressionist painter Jackson Pollock (1912–56), one of America's most famous artists, was born in Cody, Wyoming. He is known for huge paintings created by dripping and pouring paint onto the canvas from a can.

Writers created legends of the heroic cowboy. *The Virginian* by Owen Wister (1860–1938) was the first epic cowboy novel. Published in 1902, it was set in Medicine Bow, Wyoming, and captured the imagination of readers all over America. It later became a Broadway play, a Hollywood movie, and a television series. Wyoming writer Mary O'Hara (1885–1980) wrote a novel about a horse, *My Friend Flicka* (in 1941), which also became a television series.

Wyoming Politicians

Francis E. Warren (1844–1929) was elected Wyoming's first governor in 1890. He served for only six weeks before being elected to be one of Wyoming's first United States senators. He served in Washington, D.C., until his death.

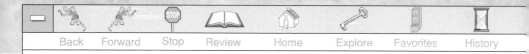

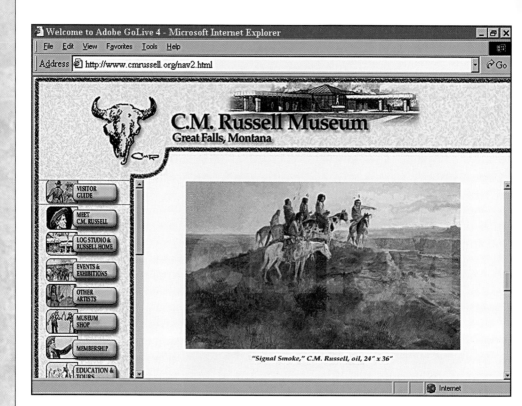

Welcome to Adobe GoLive 4 - Microsoft Internet Explorer

File   Edit   View   Favorites   Tools   Help

Address http://www.cmrussell.org/nav2.html   Go

C.M. Russell Museum
Great Falls, Montana

VISITOR GUIDE

MEET C.M. RUSSELL

LOG STUDIO & RUSSELL HOME

EVENTS & EXHIBITIONS

OTHER ARTISTS

MUSEUM SHOP

MEMBERSHIP

EDUCATION & TOURS

"Signal Smoke," C.M. Russell, oil, 24" x 36"

Internet

▲ *Charles Marion Russell had a great admiration of, and respect for American Indians, particularly those of the Northern Plains. Many of his paintings portray their way of life.*

Richard B. Cheney grew up in Casper, Wyoming, and attended the University of Wyoming. He served as a Wyoming member of the U.S. House of Representatives from 1978 until 1989, when President George H. W. Bush named him secretary of defense. He was elected vice president of the United States in 2000 under President George W. Bush.

Land and Climate

Wyoming has an area of nearly ninety-eight thousand square miles. It is bordered on the north and northwest by Montana. Idaho and Utah form the rest of Wyoming's western border. South Dakota and Nebraska lie to the east, and Colorado and Utah to the south.

▶ Wyoming's Three Regions

Wyoming has three basic land regions: the Rocky Mountains, the Intermontane Basins, and the Great Plains. The Rocky Mountains are part of a long mountain range that extends all the way from northwestern Canada to Mexico. In Wyoming, the Rockies consist of several major ranges that run from north to south. The Bighorn Mountains in the north and the Laramie Mountains in the south form the front ranges. These ranges are a natural boundary between the plains of eastern Wyoming and the mountains and basins of central and western Wyoming. Other major mountain ranges include the Absaroka, Granite, Gros Ventre, Medicine Bow, Salt River, Sierra Madre, Snake River, Teton, and Wind River ranges.

Gannett Peak, in the Wind River Range, is at 13,804 feet, Wyoming's highest mountain. Although there are many other peaks higher than 13,000 feet, the state has an average altitude of 6,700 feet. This makes Wyoming the second-highest state after Colorado.

The Continental Divide winds through Wyoming along the rim of the Rocky Mountains. Rivers that begin

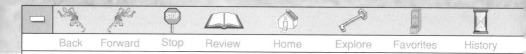
on the west side of the Divide flow toward the Pacific Ocean. Rivers on the east side of the Divide flow toward the coast of the Gulf of Mexico. Many of Wyoming's rivers are tributaries, or branches, of major rivers. West of the Divide, the Green River flows into the Colorado River in Utah. The Snake River flows through Yellowstone and Grand Teton national parks to eventually join the Columbia River. East of the Divide, the North Platte, Yellowstone, Belle Fourche, Bighorn, Sweetwater, and Powder rivers all flow into the Missouri. The Missouri eventually flows into the Mississippi, which empties into the Gulf of Mexico.

The Intermontane Basins are vast areas of flat land between the mountain ranges. *Intermontane* means "between mountains." Some of Wyoming's intermontane

▲ A map of Wyoming.

basins are called holes, such as Jackson Hole, at the base of the Teton Range. Wyoming's major basins include the Bighorn, Great Divide, Green River, Powder River and Wind River basins.

Most of Wyoming's basin lands are treeless. They are covered with short grasses and make good grazing land for cattle and sheep. Within the Great Divide Basin, midway between the towns of Rock Springs and Rawlins, is an area known as the Red Desert. Its brick-red soil stretches toward the horizon in all directions. Herds of wild horses and animals, such as pronghorn antelopes, roam this dry, empty region. They feed on sagebrush and other thinly-scattered plant growth.

The short-grass prairies of the Great Plains region in eastern Wyoming are relatively flat. In the northeastern corner of the state, the Black Hills rise from the plains to an average height of six thousand feet. These mountains appear to be black, but are actually dark green. The color comes from the ponderosa pine forests on the mountain slopes. The mountains are an extension of the famous Black Hills of South Dakota. The lowest point in Wyoming—3,099 feet above sea level—is in Crook County, not far from the Black Hills.

▶ Wyoming's Hot Spot

Yellowstone National Park is on a high plateau about 7,500 feet above sea level. The park is famous for its geysers, hot springs, fumaroles, and mud pots. Geysers form when groundwater seeps through cracks in the earth's surface down to molten volcanic rock below, and heats to the boiling point. Fumaroles are vents in the ground that shoot steam and hot gases. Bubbling mud pots, also

▲ *Yellowstone National Park is home to Old Faithful. This geyser shoots boiling water and steam 150 feet into the air about every 80 minutes.*

known as paint pots, are actually fumaroles in ponds of water.

There have been three massive volcanic eruptions at Yellowstone in the past 2 million years. Scientists believe that the eruption that occurred 2 million years ago was one of the biggest eruptions in the history of the earth. It was 2,400 times larger than the 1980 eruption of Mount St. Helens in Washington State. The most recent large eruption in Yellowstone took place 650,000 years ago. Many scientists believe that Wyoming's volcanoes will erupt again one day.

Of Bears and Bison

Until the nineteenth century, millions of buffalo, or bison, roamed the range in Wyoming, Kansas, and other parts of the Great Plains. Then the bison were hunted almost to the point of extinction. Today, the bison are back, although in smaller numbers. The high plateau of Yellowstone is home to one of the largest free-ranging bison herds in the world.

Yellowstone is one of many great places to see many of Wyoming's wild creatures. At least sixty species of mammals live in the park. There are also more than three hundred species of birds, including the bald eagle and the golden eagle. There are deer, elk, moose, and pronghorn antelope. Bighorn sheep can be seen climbing the cliffs. Yellowstone is also the home of black bears, coyotes, grizzly bears, and mountain lions. Wolves have been reintroduced into the park. Visitors to Yellowstone are advised to keep their distance from certain large wild animals: twenty-five yards from bison and elk, and at least one hundred yards from bears.

Summer Snow

Wyoming's climate is generally dry and sunny. Winters are cold and snowy. At the higher elevations, it can snow during any month of the year. Those who love to ski, toboggan, or snowshoe, will appreciate the state's fluffy, powdery snow. Some Wyomingites do not; especially those who live in isolated ranches on the plains or in the basins. Strong winds can whip up fallen snow, creating "ground" blizzards. Visibility on the ground is reduced to zero, even though the sun may be shining in a blue sky overhead. All travel by road stops in these blizzards. Wyomingites humorously say that "it only snows a couple of inches in

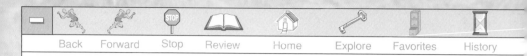

▲ One of the world's largest free-ranging bison herds roams Yellowstone National Park.

December and then the snow blows back and forth across the state the rest of the winter until it is finally worn out."[1]

Temperatures and weather conditions usually match the state's geography. Higher elevations are colder and have more snow. The average January temperature is 22°F at Casper, but only 12°F at Yellowstone Lake, which is at a higher elevation. In July, the average temperature at Casper is 71°F, while it is 59°F at Yellowstone Lake. Temperatures in winter can remain below zero for days on end. Summer temperatures in the 90s are common on the plains and in the basins. The lowest temperature ever recorded in Wyoming was –66°F at Moran on February 9, 1933. The highest temperature was 114°F at the town of Basin on July 12, 1900.

Wyoming's average annual precipitation is 13 inches. It rains or snows less on the plains, and more in the mountains. Snowfall varies from about 15 to 20 inches in the Bighorn Basin to 260 inches or more in the mountains. The Grand Targhee Ski Resort receives about 42 feet of snow in a typical winter.

Weather systems move from west to east. This means that most of the precipitation from storms falls on the western slopes of the mountains. The eastern slopes are in a "rain shadow" and receive less moisture. In summer, there are thunderstorms almost every afternoon. These storms can bring strong lightning, wind, hail, and rain. In August 1985, 6 inches of hail and 6 inches of rain combined to bury Cheyenne under giant piles of hailstones.

▲ Temperatures tend to be colder in northwestern Wyoming due to its high altitude. This mountain is located in the Yellowstone area.

Chapter 3

Economy

Wyoming is rich in coal, natural gas, oil, and other minerals. For many years, Wyoming's economy depended on these natural resources, which are used in the production of energy. This led to boom-and-bust cycles as demand for resources grew and declined. In boom cycles, when demand was growing, new businesses sprang up, and workers flocked into Wyoming. In bust cycles, when demand dropped, the industry went into a steep decline, affecting Wyoming's whole economy.

▲ *Wyoming's spacious grasslands allow for cattle and sheep to graze.*

There was an oil boom in the first three decades of the twentieth century, and again in the 1970s and early 1980s. During the 1950s, there was a uranium boom. In recent years, there has been a boom in coal mining.

Wyoming is now experiencing a boom of another sort—in tourism and service industries.

▶ A Diversified Economy

Energy resources are still an important part of the economy. In addition, Wyoming's land also provides grazing for cattle and sheep, and beautiful scenery is a resource all by itself. The growth of the tourism industry and other service industries has helped to diversify Wyoming's economy.

Service industries are the most important part of Wyoming's economy. They account for about 60 percent of the total economy and provide nearly 80 percent of the working population with jobs. In addition to tourist-related businesses, Wyoming's service industries include communications, finance, government services, real estate, retail trade, transportation, utilities, and various other types of business, community, and personal services.

Each year, more than 4 million people visit Wyoming. Tourists contribute more than $1.3 billion a year to the state's economy. Yellowstone and the soaring peaks of Grand Teton National Park are the major tourist attractions. Businesses such as hotels, ski resorts, and dude ranches all benefit from the large numbers of visitors.

There are as many as 9,200 farms and ranches in Wyoming, and the average size of a ranch is about 3,700 acres. Agriculture, though, makes up only about 2 percent of the state's economy. Only about 5 percent of Wyoming's workers are employed in agricultural jobs. Most of the state's

▲ *Devils Tower stands 1,200 feet high. President Theodore Roosevelt designated it the country's first national monument in September 1906.*

agricultural income comes from livestock production, mainly cattle ranching. The most important crops are barley, beans, hay, sugar beets, and wheat.

▶ An Energy Storehouse

A fabulous storehouse of mineral riches lies just beneath the ground in Wyoming. Mining now ranks second in importance in Wyoming's economy, accounting for 27 percent of the total. Although mining is so important, it employs only 18,600 people, or just 6 percent of Wyoming's workforce.

Wyoming is the sixth-largest producer of oil in the nation, producing 55 million barrels a year. The state is also the nation's fourth-largest producer of natural gas, producing 800 million cubic feet a year. The Overthrust Belt in southwestern Wyoming contains much of the state's reserves of oil and natural gas.

In recent years, coal has replaced oil as Wyoming's most important product. Utility companies around the country are interested in buying Wyoming's low-sulfur coal. Wyoming is the nation's largest producer of coal, producing about 300 million tons a year. Eight of the nation's ten largest coal mines are in Wyoming.

Wyoming mines are a source of many other minerals, including bentonite, sulfur, and trona, as well as the gas helium. Bentonite is a type of clay used in oil drilling and in the manufacture of certain chemical products. Trona is used in glass and chemicals such as baking soda. Sulfur is used to make many products such as fertilizer, paints, paper, shampoos, and storage batteries. Wyoming produces about 90 percent of America's supply of trona.

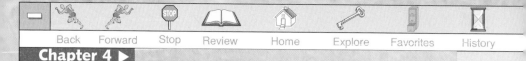
Government

On July 10, 1890, Wyoming became the forty-fourth state to be admitted to the Union. Wyoming's constitution was drafted in 1889 in preparation for statehood. The constitution outlines the structure of the state government and the powers of the various branches and departments.

▶ The Structure of Wyoming's Government

The state government is divided into three branches— legislative, executive, and judicial. The legislative branch creates the laws, which the executive branch carries out, and the judicial branch then interprets these laws.

The head of the executive branch is the governor. He or she is elected by Wyoming's voters to a four-year term of office. The governor can serve no more than two terms during a sixteen-year period. Four other officials of the executive branch—the secretary of state, superintendent of public instruction, auditor, and treasurer—are elected by the voters. Their terms of office are also limited to eight years in a sixteen-year period. The governor appoints other important state officials, such as the attorney general, members of the state board of education, and the heads of many other state agencies. Unlike many other states, Wyoming's executive branch does not have a lieutenant governor. If the governor cannot complete his or her term, the secretary of state serves as governor until a new governor is elected.

The legislative branch of Wyoming's government consists of a thirty-member senate and a sixty-member house of representatives. Senators are elected to four-year terms. They are limited to three terms during a twenty-four-year period. Representatives are elected to two-year terms and can serve no more than six terms during a twenty-four-year period.

The judicial branch consists of the state supreme court, nine district courts, and twenty-three county courts. There are also various police courts, municipal courts, and justice of the peace courts. The governor appoints all judges of the supreme court and district courts. The five supreme court

WOW Museum: Western Women's Suffrage - Wyoming - Microsoft Internet Explorer

File Edit View Favorites Tools Help

Address http://www.womenofthewest.org/exhibits/suffrage/justice_full.html   Go

WOMEN OF THE WEST
museum

Suffrage Home   Timeline   Credits
Biographies   Activities   Resources

California | Colorado | Hawaii
Kansas | New Mexico | Oregon
Texas | Utah | Washington | Wyoming

Timeline

1869- William Bright sponsors suffrage bill before Wyoming Territorial Legislature; Governor John A. Campbell signs bill approving full suffrage for women.

Esther Hobart Morris (1814-1902), Wyoming suffragist and Sweetwater County Justice of the Peace.
Denver Public Library, Western History/Genealogy Department

http://www.womenofthewest.org/exhibits/suffrage/index.html   Internet

▲ *Esther Hobart Morris was an antislavery and women's rights activist who helped Wyoming become the first government in the world to grant women the vote. This work led to her appointment as the first woman in Wyoming and the United States to serve as justice of the peace.*

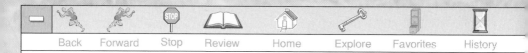
justices serve eight-year terms. The nine district courts each have one or two judges, who serve six-year terms. In the election following the appointment of a judge, voters get to decide whether the judge stays in office.

▶ The Equality State

Wyoming became a United States territory in 1868. In 1869, the first territorial legislature passed a law granting women many political privileges. They could vote, be elected to office, and serve on juries. Wyoming was the first place in the United States to give women equal rights. This is why the official state motto is "Equal Rights," and the state nickname is "The Equality State."

In 1870, women in Wyoming served on juries. In the same year, Esther Hobart Morris (1814–1902) was appointed justice of the peace for the South Pass District. Morris became the first woman in America to hold such a position. Although her involvement in the struggle for equal rights for women is disputed, she did become a symbol for the movement. There is a statue of her in front of the state capitol building in Cheyenne. Inscribed on the statue are these words: "Esther Hobart Morris, proponent of the legislative act which in 1869 gave distinction to the territory of Wyoming as the 1st government in the world to grant women equal rights."[1]

In the governor's office in the capitol building is a portrait of Nellie Tayloe Ross (1876–1977). Ross took over as governor of Wyoming when her husband, Governor William Ross, suddenly died in office. Nellie Ross was nominated to replace him, and she won a special election. She thus became the first woman to be inaugurated as a state governor in the United States. She served from 1925 to 1927.

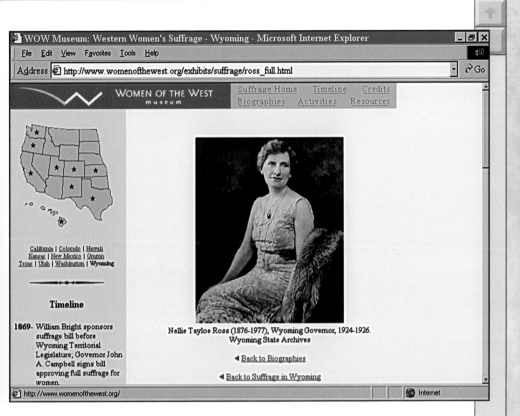

WOW Museum: Western Women's Suffrage - Wyoming - Microsoft Internet Explorer

File　Edit　View　Favorites　Tools　Help

Address　http://www.womenofthewest.org/exhibits/suffrage/ross_full.html　Go

WOMEN OF THE WEST
m u s e u m

Suffrage Home　Timeline　Credits
Biographies　Activities　Resources

California | Colorado | Hawaii
Kansas | New Mexico | Oregon
Texas | Utah | Washington | Wyoming

Timeline

1869- William Bright sponsors
suffrage bill before
Wyoming Territorial
Legislature; Governor John
A. Campbell signs bill
approving full suffrage for
women.

Nellie Tayloe Ross (1876-1977), Wyoming Governor, 1924-1926.
Wyoming State Archives

◀ Back to Biographies

◀ Back to Suffrage in Wyoming

http://www.womenofthewest.org/　　　Internet

▲ Nellie Tayloe Ross was America's first female governor.

Wyomingites are proud of their state's historical status as "The Equality State." Perhaps that is why they seem to take their right to vote more seriously than do voters in many other states. For example, in the 2000 presidential election Wisconsin voters turned out at the fourth highest percentage in the nation.

Chapter 5

History

The very first people to set foot in what is now Wyoming were groups of nomadic hunters who arrived sometime before 9000 B.C. They were descendants of nomadic peoples from Asia who had followed herds of wild animals across a bridge of land connecting Siberia and Alaska.

▶ Wyoming's Earliest Inhabitants

Scientists have learned much about Wyoming's earliest inhabitants, known as Paleo-Indians. The evidence points to a life based on hunting large game. Stone spear points have been found among the bones of mammoth and bison. Scientists date these animal remains at about 9000 B.C. Stone arrowheads, knives, axes, and various kinds of scrapers have also been found.

There are other signs of the Paleo-Indians' existence. In the Bighorn Mountains, near the town of Sheridan, Wyoming, there is a huge circle of stones on the ground. Twenty-eight lines of stones radiate outward from a pile of stones at the center of the circle. The purpose of this circle, known as the Medicine Wheel, is a mystery. Scientists wonder if it stood for the sun and the phases of the moon. They believe it probably was part of a religious ritual. Wyoming's ancient inhabitants also left petroglyphs and pictographs on canyon walls. Petroglyphs are images carved into stone, while pictographs are images painted on the stone.

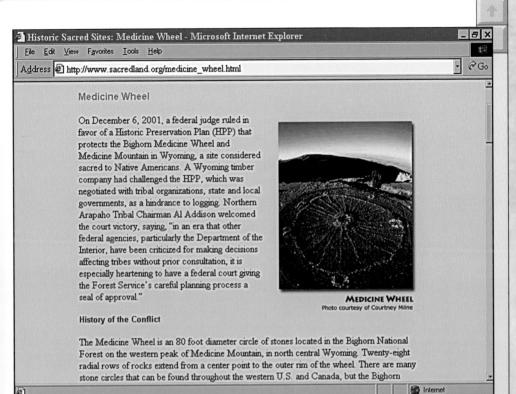

Historic Sacred Sites: Medicine Wheel - Microsoft Internet Explorer

File   Edit   View   Favorites   Tools   Help

Address   http://www.sacredland.org/medicine_wheel.html   Go

Medicine Wheel

On December 6, 2001, a federal judge ruled in favor of a Historic Preservation Plan (HPP) that protects the Bighorn Medicine Wheel and Medicine Mountain in Wyoming, a site considered sacred to Native Americans. A Wyoming timber company had challenged the HPP, which was negotiated with tribal organizations, state and local governments, as a hindrance to logging. Northern Arapaho Tribal Chairman Al Addison welcomed the court victory, saying, "in an era that other federal agencies, particularly the Department of the Interior, have been criticized for making decisions affecting tribes without prior consultation, it is especially heartening to have a federal court giving the Forest Service's careful planning process a seal of approval."

MEDICINE WHEEL
Photo courtesy of Courtney Milne

History of the Conflict

The Medicine Wheel is an 80 foot diameter circle of stones located in the Bighorn National Forest on the western peak of Medicine Mountain, in north central Wyoming. Twenty-eight radial rows of rocks extend from a center point to the outer rim of the wheel. There are many stone circles that can be found throughout the western U.S. and Canada, but the Bighorn

Internet

The Medicine Wheel is located on the western peak of Medicine Mountain. It is considered to be an altar for the mountain, which is of spiritual significance to many American Indian tribes, including the Cheyenne and Lakota.

▷ American Indians of Wyoming

For thousands of years, the descendants of the Paleo-Indians continued to wander, following herds of bison across the plains and basins. By the 1800s, different tribal groups of American Indians occupied various parts of Wyoming. The Sioux lived in the Powder River Basin; the Crow were in the Bighorn Basin; and the Cheyenne and Arapaho were south of the North Platte River. The Shoshone and Bannock had moved from the Great Basin into the Green River and Wind River valleys. The Ute

lived in the Sierra Madre Mountains and in the deserts of western Wyoming. Although the tribes spoke different languages, they communicated through a commonly understood sign language.

The arrival of Europeans in the West brought many changes for these tribes. One was the introduction of the horse. The Spanish first brought horses to New Mexico in the 1600s. Probably as early as 1700, Wyoming's Shoshone obtained horses through trading. Horses made it much easier for Wyoming's native peoples to follow the bison herds. Food became much more plentiful, and the American Indian population grew rapidly. Rivalries between tribes also grew, with raiding parties frequently attacking other tribes, often to steal horses.

Explorers, Trappers, and Traders

Two brothers from French Canada—François and Louis-Joseph La Vérendrye—may have been the first Europeans to set eyes on Wyoming, in about 1743. Other French explorers followed them, trapping beaver and fox or trading for fur with the American Indians. In 1803, President Thomas Jefferson paid France $15 million for a vast territory west of the Mississippi, including the eastern portion of Wyoming. This event was called the Louisiana Purchase, which doubled the size of the United States.

Jefferson was eager to learn more about America's new lands. In 1804, Meriwether Lewis and William Clark led an expedition to the West. A Shoshone woman named Sacajawea (1786–1812) served as their guide and transla-tor. The expedition reached the Pacific Coast in 1805. On the return journey, John Colter left the expedition to explore the Rocky Mountains. In 1807 and 1808, he wan-dered through the Yellowstone region of northwestern

Wyoming, hoping to develop a fur trade with the Crow Indians.

In the early 1800s, fur hats and cloaks were very fashionable and brought high prices on the East Coast and in Europe. In 1812, Robert Stuart led a group sponsored by the Pacific Fur Company. It was they who discovered South Pass, a relatively easy route over the Continental Divide, which became part of the Oregon Trail. Within ten years, fur trappers were searching for beaver and other fur-bearing animals throughout the mountains. Known as "mountain men," the trappers often asked the American Indians for help in trapping beaver and stretching and drying the pelts. Once a year, the mountain men would come together for an event known as the *rendezvous,* or "gathering." They would trade furs,

▲ *Francois and Louis-Joseph La Vérendrye were the first Europeans to see Wyoming's untapped beauty.*

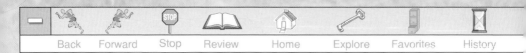
ammunition, food, and other supplies. They would also swap stories and information.

By 1840, fur items had fallen out of fashion, and Wyoming's mountain men had to find other sources of income. Some became guides for the military or government expeditions. Others became guides for settlers heading west. A trapper named Jim Bridger (1804–81) had explored much of Wyoming in 1823 and 1824. He became a scout for the U.S. Army. In 1843, Bridger and his partner, Louis Vasquez, established Fort Bridger in southwestern Wyoming.

Another U.S. Army scout, John C. Frémont (1813–90), mapped various routes across Wyoming and explored the Wind River Mountains. Fur traders William Sublette and Robert Campbell established Fort William in eastern Wyoming in 1834. It became the first permanent trading post in the area. The fort's name was later changed to Fort Laramie.

▶ The Road West

The fur trappers were the first white men to use the Oregon Trail in Wyoming. South Pass became the preferred route through the mountains. By 1830, wagons carrying furs and supplies were crossing Wyoming. By the 1840s, settlers from the east followed in the footsteps of the fur trappers on their way to the Pacific Northwest. At first, only a few pioneers were brave enough to risk the dangerous overland journey. Then, each year their numbers increased.

In 1847, Mormons began traveling along the Oregon Trail through Wyoming. At Fort Bridger, beyond South Pass, the Mormons left the Oregon Trail and followed another route to Utah. In 1849, a new stream of travelers

▲ *The Oregon Trail was 1,932 miles long, beginning in Independence, Missouri, and ending in Oregon City.*

moved across Wyoming. Gold had been discovered in California the previous year, and the Forty-Niners headed west hoping to make fortunes.

During the earliest years of westward migration along the Oregon Trail, relations between the whites and American Indians were generally friendly. The American Indians traded with the travelers and often provided useful information about grazing lands and watering spots. As the flood of immigrants increased, conflicts arose. The American Indians complained that the newcomers were trampling the grass, polluting the water, spreading disease,

causing prairie fires, and killing the bison. Fighting broke out, and the U.S. Army often had to intervene to restore order. Most battles resulted in many more casualties among the American Indians than among the United States soldiers. Several peace treaties were signed but never honored.

▶ Indian Wars

Until the mid-1860s, huge herds of buffalo continued to roam Wyoming's grasslands. At the time, a settler named William D. Street described a buffalo herd in the Wind River Valley: "The herd was not less than 20 miles in width—we never saw the other side—at least 60 miles in length, maybe much longer; two counties of buffaloes! There might have been 100,000, or 1,000,000, or 100,000,000. I don't know."[1]

During the 1860s, the Union Pacific railroad was being built across Wyoming. The company hired buffalo hunters to supply fresh meat for the small army of railroad workers. The American Indians saw this new hunting of the bison as a threat to their way of life.

Another source of conflict developed during the 1860s when gold was discovered in Montana. Settlers and gold seekers on their way to Montana followed the Bozeman Trail across northeastern Wyoming. This trail crossed the Powder River Basin, the home of the Sioux. The U.S. Army built Fort Phil Kearny near the Bighorn Mountains to protect these travelers. Sioux Chief Red Cloud led his warriors in battles against the army. The fighting stopped when the army agreed to abandon the fort. The American Indians, in turn, agreed not to interfere with the building of the railroad in southern Wyoming.

Then, during the 1870s, gold was discovered in the Black Hills. The Sioux considered this land sacred. White

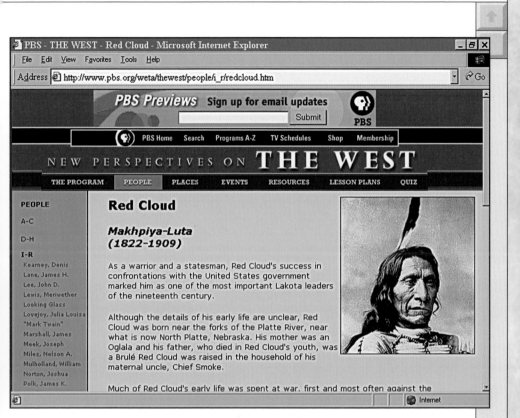

PBS Previews Sign up for email updates

Submit

PBS

PBS Home   Search   Programs A-Z   TV Schedules   Shop   Membership

NEW PERSPECTIVES ON **THE WEST**

THE PROGRAM   PEOPLE   PLACES   EVENTS   RESOURCES   LESSON PLANS   QUIZ

PEOPLE
A-C
D-H
I-R
Kearney, Denis
Lane, James H.
Lee, John D.
Lewis, Meriwether
Looking Glass
Lovejoy, Julia Louisa
"Mark Twain"
Marshall, James
Meek, Joseph
Miles, Nelson A.
Mulholland, William
Norton, Joshua
Polk, James K.

Red Cloud

Makhpiya-Luta
(1822-1909)

As a warrior and a statesman, Red Cloud's success in confrontations with the United States government marked him as one of the most important Lakota leaders of the nineteenth century.

Although the details of his early life are unclear, Red Cloud was born near the forks of the Platte River, near what is now North Platte, Nebraska. His mother was an Oglala and his father, who died in Red Cloud's youth, was a Brulé Red Cloud was raised in the household of his maternal uncle, Chief Smoke.

Much of Red Cloud's early life was spent at war, first and most often against the

Internet

▲ *Red Cloud's strategies against the United States were the most successful of any American Indian nation. This skill led to the Fort Laramie Treaty, which required the United States to abandon its posts along the Bozeman Trail.*

settlers flooded into the area, eager to find gold. Once again the American Indians attacked. On June 25, 1876, forces led by Crazy Horse and Sitting Bull defeated Colonel George A. Custer and his troops at the Battle of Little Bighorn. The U.S. Army was now determined to drive the American Indians off their lands. Within five years, the last of the tribes had given up the fight and were forced onto reservations.

Most of the battles between American Indians and the new settlers in Wyoming involved the Arapaho, Cheyenne,

and Sioux. The Shoshone, under Chief Washakie, had always remained peaceful. Still, the Shoshone were forced onto the Wind River Reservation. Chief Washakie described the sad fate of his people: "And so, at last, our fathers were steadily driven out, or killed, and we, their sons, but sorry remnants of tribes once mighty, are cornered in little spots of the earth all ours of right—cornered like guilty prisoners, and watched by men with guns, who are more than anxious to kill us off."[2]

Among the white settlers who fought the American Indians was William F. Cody, better known as Buffalo Bill. In 1883, Buffalo Bill organized his Wild West Show, which traveled all over the United States and Europe for

▲ William F. Cody, otherwise known as Buffalo Bill, organized a touring show in 1883. Custer's Last Stand was a feature presentation.

twenty years. The show depicted Western life for huge, enthusiastic audiences. Among the stars were Sitting Bull and sharpshooter Annie Oakley. Buffalo Bill expressed a deep sympathy for the plight of the American Indians:

> In nine cases out of ten when there is trouble between white men and Indians, it will be found that the white man is responsible. . . . The defeat of Custer was not a massacre. The Indians were being pursued by skilled fighters with orders to kill. For centuries they had been hounded from the Atlantic to the Pacific and back again. They had their wives and little ones to protect and they were fighting for their existence.[3]

The town of Cody, Wyoming, at the eastern entrance to Yellowstone National Park, is named after Buffalo Bill. Each year, more than three hundred thousand people visit the Buffalo Bill Historical Center, also located in Cody.

The Wild West

By 1867, the Union Pacific Railroad reached as far west as present-day Cheyenne. By 1869, the final link of the transcontinental railroad was completed at Promontory Point in Utah. Soon the "iron horse" was chugging back and forth across Wyoming. Cheyenne became a bustling town, as more and more people flocked to the state. Evanston, Green River, Laramie, Rawlins, Rock Springs, and other towns sprang up along the railroad route.

The completion of the railroad brought an end to travel along the Oregon Trail. The difficult six-month journey could now be made in relative comfort in a matter of days. An estimated 375,000 men, women, and children had made the westward trek along the Oregon Trail in the years before the railroad arrived.

During the 1870s and 1880s, Wyoming became a land of cowboys. There were few bison left on the plains, so

Wyoming grassland was available for grazing cattle. After the first cattle drive through Wyoming, in 1866, the numbers grew steadily. By 1884, there were as many as eight hundred thousand cattle on the range in Wyoming.

During these years, Wyoming became typical of the "Wild West." Gangs of outlaws rustled cattle, held up stagecoaches, and robbed banks. Gunslingers hired them-selves out to the highest bidder. Wyoming's most famous outlaw was Butch Cassidy (born George Leroy Parker). Cassidy was the leader of the Hole-in-the-Wall gang. The gang members, including Harry Longabaugh (known as the Sundance Kid) liked to call themselves the "Wild

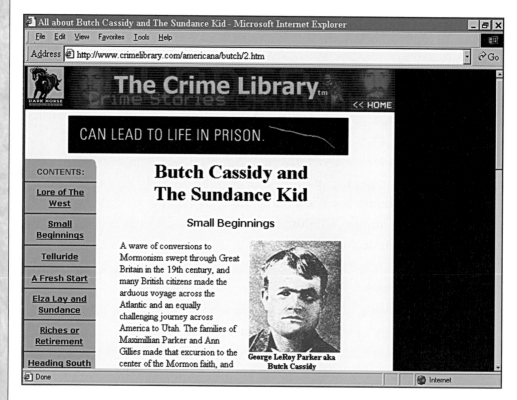

All about Butch Cassidy and The Sundance Kid - Microsoft Internet Explorer

File   Edit   View   Favorites   Tools   Help

Address http://www.crimelibrary.com/americana/butch/2.htm

The Crime Library.tm

<< HOME

CAN LEAD TO LIFE IN PRISON.

CONTENTS:

Lore of The West

Small Beginnings

Telluride

A Fresh Start

Elza Lay and Sundance

Riches or Retirement

Heading South

Butch Cassidy and The Sundance Kid

Small Beginnings

A wave of conversions to Mormonism swept through Great Britain in the 19th century, and many British citizens made the arduous voyage across the Atlantic and an equally challenging journey across America to Utah. The families of Maximillian Parker and Ann Gillies made that excursion to the center of the Mormon faith, and

George LeRoy Parker aka Butch Cassidy

Done   Internet

Butch Cassidy became an American legend as an outlaw. Cassidy and his gang, the Wild Bunch, were best known for their bank and train heists.

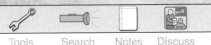
Bunch." One of Cassidy's hideouts was located near the town of Kaycee, Wyoming.

Problems persisted on the plains, and range wars broke out between the wealthy cattle owners and the small ranchers. The cattle barons were determined to stop rustling. They were also unhappy when small ranchers and homesteaders began fencing their properties, because the fences stopped the large herds from grazing freely. In 1892, wealthy members of the Wyoming Stock Growers Association (WSGA) took the law into their own hands. They hired a gang of gunmen from Texas to frighten—and if need be murder—small ranchers and cattle rustlers in Johnson County. There was little bloodshed in the dispute known as the Johnson County War—only two men on each side were killed. The arrival of the United States cavalry prevented further fighting. The cattle barons and their gunmen were not brought to trial despite their illegal actions.

Conflicts later broke out between Wyoming's cattlemen and sheep owners. The sheep and cattle competed for the same grazing lands on the open range. By 1902, there were almost 6 million sheep on the range in Wyoming. During the early 1900s, some of Wyoming's sheepherders were murdered by cattlemen.

▶ A Century of Progress

Early in the twentieth century, cowboys continued to ride the range and there were still many sheepherders tending to their flocks. Wyoming's population grew as farmers arrived to take advantage of free land and new irrigation projects. Drought and declining prices, however, hurt farms, and mining outpaced agriculture to become the main economic force.

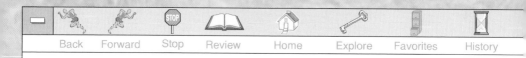
The oil industry developed at the beginning of the twentieth century. The town of Casper was the center of Wyoming's first oil boom during the 1910s. During the 1920s, Wyoming's Teapot Dome oil field, north of Casper, was at the center of a huge national political scandal. This field was controlled by the federal government. Albert Fall, President Warren G. Harding's secretary of the interior, accepted between $100,000 and $400,000 in bribes to lease Teapot Dome to his oil-business buddies, Harry F. Sinclair and Edward L. Doheney. Fall was convicted of bribery and sentenced to prison. Wyoming's economy slipped as public confidence was shaken. Many of the state's banks failed, even before the national economic collapse that came with the Great Depression in the 1930s.

▲ Wyomingites are trying to preserve the natural beauty of their state by protecting it against pollution.

During the Depression, oil production actually increased in Wyoming. Further progress came with the construction of new dams on the North Platte River. The dams provided water for irrigation of farmland and for hydroelectric power.

When the United States entered World War II in 1941, Wyoming's economy rebounded with the increased demand for natural resources. After the war ended in 1945, an increase in tourism brought new prosperity. Later, during the Arab oil embargo of 1973–74, the price of oil skyrocketed. Wyoming benefited hugely. The state's population shot up 42 percent during the 1970s. In the 1980s, the demand for oil decreased once again, and the economy suffered. However, by this time, Wyoming's economy was more diversified. Recovery was soon under way, with new growth in service industries, tourism, and resources such as coal.

Environmental issues are important in Wyoming, today. Increasing numbers of tourists mean more traffic and air pollution. The use of snowmobiles in the national parks is under constant review. The snowmobiles not only cause air and noise pollution, but can also be a threat to wildlife. How to manage the forests and handle forest fires is also an area of much discussion.

Today, Wyomingites look forward to a promising future as they continue to pay tribute to their past. Annual events, such as the Mountain Men Rendezvous, the Old West Days festival near Jackson, and Cheyenne's Frontier Days, are reminders of the state's colorful frontier days.

Chapter 1. The State of Wyoming

1. Nathaniel Burt, *Wyoming* (New York: Fodor's Travel Publications, 1995), p. 208.

2. Ibid.

Chapter 2. Land and Climate

1. Don Pitcher, *Wyoming Handbook* (Emeryville, Calif.: Avalon Travel Publishing, Inc., 2000), p. 6.

Chapter 4. Government

1. Nathaniel Burt, *Wyoming* (New York: Fodor's Travel Publications, 1995), p. 42.

2. NCSL, "2000 Voter Turnout," *National Conference of State Legislatures*, n.d., <http://www.ncsl.org/programs/legman/elect/00voterturn.htm> (October 15, 2002).

Chapter 5. History

1. Don Pitcher, *Wyoming Handbook* (Emeryville, Calif.: Avalon Travel Publishing, 2000), p. 12.

2. Ibid., p. 18. (*Chief Washakie*, quoted in Chief Washakie by Mae Urbanek, Boulder, Colo.: Johnson Publishing Co., 1971—out of print).

3. Nathaniel Burt, *Wyoming* (New York: Fodor's Travel Publications, 1995), p. 196.

Further Reading

Baldwin, Guy. *Wyoming*. Tarrytown, N.Y.: Marshall Cavendish Corporation, 1999.

Burt, Nathaniel. *Wyoming*. New York: Fodor's Travel Publications, 1995.

Fradin, Dennis Brindell, and Judith Bloom Fradin. *Wyoming*. Chicago: Children's Press, 1994.

Frisch, Carlienne. *Wyoming*. Minneapolis, Minn.: Lerner Publishing Company, 1994.

Kent, Deborah. *Yellowstone National Park*. Chicago: Children's Press, 1994.

———., *Wyoming*. Danbury, Conn.: Children's Press, 2000.

Marsh, Carole. *Wyoming Facts and Factivities*. Peachtree City, Ga.: Gallopade International, 1996.

Pitcher, Don. *Wyoming Handbook*. Emeryville, Calif.: Avalon Travel Publishing, 2000.

Steffof, Rebecca. *The Oregon Trail in American History*. Berkeley Heights, N.J.: Enslow Publishers, Inc., 1997.

Thompson, Kathleen. *Wyoming*. Austin, Tex.: Raintree Steck-Vaughn Publishers, 1996.